Th _____ , ____

in Babylon

Seven Simple Rules to Wealth

M. A. Haley, Ph.D.

Cover designed by jeweldesign

This book is a work of the author's personal experiences. Any resemblance to other actual persons, living or dead, events, or locales is entirely coincidental.

M. A. Haley, Ph.D.
Visit my website at www.RichestMom.com

Printed in the United States of America

First Printing: October 2018
M. A. Haley, LLC

ISBN-9781720184355
Independently Published

To my daughter Jenna, who inspires me every single day.
And to Kurt, the reason I have come so far, so fast.

I love you both so much.

Matthew 19:26

Money is plentiful for those who understand the simple
rules of its acquisition.

.   —GEORGE S. CLASON

Contents

Introduction

The fact that you're not where
you want to be should be
motivation enough.
— The Universe

I WROTE THIS BOOK BECAUSE a few short years ago, my financial world was rocked. Yet from that rubble, I built a net worth of $50,000 and then in 5 short years turned it into $500,000. That accomplishment was a big deal, but sharing that accomplishment is a bigger deal. If I can do this, ANYONE CAN. But let me start at the beginning … the beginning of the end.

After 17 years of matrimony, I divorced. I walked away with my dignity, a 6-year-old daughter, and an ever-growing pile of debt. For a lot of reasons, (including amazing independence and ridiculous stubbornness), I took no spouse or child support. And as a soon-to-be divorcee, I quickly learned that creditors who once adored me suddenly labeled me "high risk." My own credit union that I started membership at age 15 wouldn't give me a cent of credit despite my high 700-FICO score.

As a single mom, I felt isolated, overwhelmed, and embarrassed. Savings was on the back-burner, and retirement slipped beyond my financial event horizon. I telescoped my big old ostrich head into the sand and I wasn't coming up for air anytime soon. I couldn't deal with my financial situation, so I didn't.

Then, 18 months later, my job and sole source of income took a big hit. My hours and salary were cut by 10%. I felt like I'd been working so hard to stay afloat, that this could be the iceberg that takes us down. It could have been a catastrophe. Fortunately, it became the jolt I needed to pop my head out of the sand. One look around, and I knew I was lost. Rather than panicking, I took a breath and assessed my money matters.

I took control of my situation before it took control of me. What I did during that time was monumental. By following what I now call 7 Simple Rules of Wealth, I was able to keep what I had and build the foundation for wealth accumulation.

Eventually, my salary and hours returned to normal, but my mindset was forever changed. It enabled me to quadruple my cash and investments in the first 3 years. I went from a net worth of $50,000 to $500,000 in 5 years. I paid off all my credit cards. I charged down a path to pay off my house and simultaneously set myself up for a nice retirement. It blessed me to provide for my special needs daughter and equally set up her future.

So how did it happen? Could anyone do this? There was a combination of factors that contributed to this phenomenal outcome, but it all began with me taking the first steps. The steps I developed were thought out and deliberate. But these steps apparently weren't original. As I began building, I wanted to learn as much as possible to see if I could achieve more, faster. I happened upon an old lecture by Jim Rohn, a self-made multi-millionaire and renowned motivational speaker.

In one of his lectures captured on YouTube, he said that his biggest recommendation to everyone in his lectures is to read 'The Richest Man in Babylon'. He followed this by stating that very few people did and consequently never became millionaires. Really? I mean, if a millionaire says 'read this and you'll be a millionaire' why wouldn't people do that? The next day, I checked it out of the library.

To my surprise, I happened to do everything recommended in 'The Richest Man in Babylon.' That really worried me because the steps I took seemed to me to come to me, but not instantly or apparently. Each step was essential in taking me from point A to point B, but it was far from intuitive. Some steps came from financially savvy friends. Others steps I found in articles, books, and the internet. What if I hadn't discovered those steps? What if I hadn't done those steps at all? If I had read this book, could I be richer faster?
So, if all this financial advice was at the fingertips of anyone with a library card, why isn't everyone a millionaire? Why hadn't I discovered it sooner? Well, for one, this iconic book wasn't exactly marketed to women, let alone single moms.

I knew 'The Richest Man in Babylon' the same way one knows about 'Don Quixote' or 'War and Peace' ... we've all heard about them, but how many of us have actually read them or know what they're about? Looking at the title, I would have never even considered this book.

Think about it; can the richest man of an ancient and 'extinct' empire actually teach me something about my finances today? Yet the truth remained -- these teachings in whatever form are quintessential to the accumulation of wealth and a lifestyle of abundance.

Seeing how this blueprint unburdened me, I wondered if it could lift the weight of other hard working, struggling moms. I was inspired with passion. I needed to share this information, but in a way that moms everywhere could take it in, hold it close, and dramatically change their lives forever. I wrote this book for each and every one of you reading it now. And for you I wish you an amazing journey ahead.

Embrace your path to wealth. You've got this!

But Why Babylon

*Proper preparation is the key
to our success. Our acts can
be no wiser than our
thoughts. Our thinking can
be no wiser than our
understanding.*
— *George S. Clason*

N 1926, GEORGE S. CLASON wrote *The Richest Man in Babylon*, which today is considered a classic and has sold over 2 million copies worldwide. Even so, I hadn't heard about it until one of my favorite speakers, Jim Rohn, credited that book to making him a millionaire by age 32. (He also mentioned that although he always recommends it, less than 10% of his audience would actually bother to pick it up.) I picked it up and read it and wondered 'why Babylon'?

Clason seemed to choose Babylon because it was an ancient Mesopotamian city known for abundance. People lived lavishly. Excess was the name of the game. Days were casual and evenings were carefree. But Babylon didn't begin that way as it was a miserable terrain to master. There were no natural trade routes. Water, even in the form of rain, was scarce. The Babylonians overcame their setbacks through persistence and creativity. (Just as to become a millionaire in one lifetime you also need persistence and creativity.)

All the resources to transform and sustain Babylon were developed by its citizens, and all their riches were born of sheer determination. Eventually, the Babylonians left, and so left their paradise in the desert. Today it sits hot and dry in a desolate part of Asia just 30-degrees above the equator; it parallels the climate of Yuma, Arizona. This nearly undiscoverable wasteland bears no resemblance to glory days. The only evidence of its existence lay in an excavation site, giving archaeologists a glimpse of a puzzle; a wondrous civilization whose splendors seem unachievable by any civilization, let alone an ancient one.

If we crack open a page from their history, we find the ancient Babylonians were educated. Enlightened. They had a written history.

In fact, they had one of the oldest written histories dating back 8000 years. Among them were engineers, astronomers, and mathematicians. But their greatest achievements were with their financiers, who discovered the secrets to wealth and abundance.

Those secrets, preserved in stone tablets, were discovered in a serendipitous excavation, leading to a remarkable translation hosted by a generous cadre of benefactors who believed the knowledge should be owned by all.

This wisdom of Babylon endures. Their secrets to wealth and abundance lay before you.

∞∞∞∞

My Fundamentals of Money:

Money is a tool by which success is measured, and makes possible enjoyment of the best the world affords.

Money is abundant for those who understand the simple laws which govern its acquisition.

Money is governed today by the same laws which controlled it on the prosperous streets of Babylon, thousands of years ago.

The Seven Simple Rules of Wealth

Financial freedom is a mental, emotional and educational process.
— Robert Kiyosaki, Net Worth $85 Million

THE SEVEN SIMPLE RULES OF WEALTH are just that … simple. You don't need to know how to read a profit and loss statement, or take an accounting class. These rules are intuitive and build upon each other. You also don't have to do them all, BUT doing them together magnifies the outcome and gets you there faster. The rules will be detailed in the next chapters, but are:

1. Fill Your Purse
2. Spend with a Sanity Check

3. Make your Money Multiply

4. Guard your Stash

5. Make your House Profitable

6. Focus on your Future Self

7. Increase your Earnings

I know this little list doesn't look like much. But take it from this single working mom who went from a net worth of $50,000 to half a million dollars in under 5 years that this is mind-blowingly, earth-shatteringly B-I-G. This isn't a get-rich-quick scheme. This is your own personal get-rich-quick-smart challenge. People have used these techniques over and over again through the centuries to unbelievable success. I've done it. You can too.

∞◌◌◌∞

"I always knew I was going to be rich. I don't think I ever doubted it for a minute." - Warren Buffett, Net Worth at age 21: $20,000*

[*Note: Just to be clear, $20,000 in 1951 was nothing to sneeze at. At the time, it could have bought two-and-a-half new houses, and was roughly six times the average household income. But he's still one of the richest people in the world today, so you get my point.]

Rule 1: Fill Your Purse

If you don't get serious about your money, You will never have serious money.
— Grant Cardone, Net Worth $355 Million

HAVE YOU EVER FELT YOUR PURSE OVERFLOWING with everything but money? I have for much longer than I care to admit. I actually used to write checks for individual postage stamps. (Seriously, in the 90's what was a postage stamp, like 27 cents?) I charged groceries, haircuts, gas, and everything I possibly could to credit cards because I didn't have the money to afford the basics. Looking back, I'm really grateful that mortgages and auto payments can't be made with credit cards. Nothing compounds debt like interest on interest. And you know what? It was exhausting and stressful, and I desperately wanted a different life. But getting a different life required a whole new focus. Me. And not in the way that most people say "I deserve it. I deserve to buy all this stuff on credit. I focused on me by paying myself first. Paying yourself first isn't a just strategy to cover everyday expenses, but the key to abundance and wealth.

PAY YOURSELF FIRST ... IT'S THE KEY TO ABUNDANCE AND WEALTH

Think of cash as your partner. Your very attractive, super-high-maintenance, ready to leave you at a moment's notice partner. If you want to keep your partner, (and trust me when I say this is a partner you want to keep) you have to work excruciatingly hard each and every day on building your relationship. Cash demands attention at every turn, and its patience is fleeting. If you aren't loyal to your cash, it won't be loyal to you. It'll just as easily maintain a relationship with someone else ... anyone else ... who will give it the attention it deserves. Perhaps your cash's wondering eye is spying heading toward a handbag salesperson. Maybe it's itching to hitch a ride to the next Amazon seller.

(My cash has decent standards with Amazon sellers, only lured by those with at least 4 stars, so I have to really work to keep it!) Don't neglect your cash away. Start paying attention and watch it build.

And by the way, cash tends to build quickly and easily. Start with this simple task: for every 10 dollars you have, spend no more than 9. And by extension, for every 100 dollars you have, spend no more than 90. You've probably caught on that we're focused on 10%, but why? Because over time, if you do this each and every time, your purse will start to fill. Before long, it will overflow. On the flip side, so long as you don't give away more than 90% of your money, your riches will grow. Simple, right?

FILL YOUR PURSE BY GIVING AWAY LESS THAN 90% OF YOUR MONEY - KEEP 10%

Not that I'm saying you're frivolously GIVING it away. But every time you pay for something, whether it's a utility bill or a frothy cappuccino, you ARE giving it away. Some of this handover is in exchange for needs. Some for wants. But either way, you're handing over cash in exchange for a thing, a taste, an experience, in any myriad of manifestations. Granted, that 'experience' might be princess pleasures like indoor plumbing and WIFI, but every dollar going out counts. Needs and wants are paid by the exact same pot of money. Your pot of money. Everything absolutely, positively counts. If it all counts, then to get control you have to count it all. Counting it all is the only way you can understand where the 90% ends and the 10% starts. That 10% is yours. That 10% is important and powerful. The least you deserve for all your hard work and ceaselessly putting others before yourself is 10% of your own money.

THE LEAST YOU DESERVE FOR ALL YOUR HARD WORK IS 10% OF YOUR OWN MONEY

But what if you're really crunched and you just can't do it? The cash has to go out. Bills have to be paid, right? Good news! My experience with money is that it's worth more than its face value. It can be stretched. It can buy more than the straight 90% it looks like. Sometimes it can buy so much more. Follow my lead and spend a little extra time finding ways to keep at least 10% of your money by making your 90% worth the full 100%, (or $90 worth $100). This way, keeping 10% isn't a burden — it's a bonus.

MAKE YOUR 90% WORTH THE WHOLE 100%

How can we get close to making a dollar out of fifteen cents? Let's just say that most things in life is negotiable. She who negotiates best wins! I know the sheer discomfort of negotiating, but your money is on the line. Each and every opportunity to negotiate is an opportunity to increase the value of your 90%. A dollar here, ten dollars there quickly adds up. And by the way, everyone pays a different price for the exact same thing. Ask yourself this; if everyone pays a different price for the exact same thing, do you want to be paying more or paying less? If you want a purse overflowing with cash, get better at negotiating. It's not easy. Even after all these years, my intuition is to not negotiate. But then I ask myself if I want to pay less or more than the next person. It makes an unbelievably HUGE difference in how much of my money I get to keep. Oh, and negotiating on little things has helped me negotiate really big things, from airfare to hotels, to buying cars and houses. I'm also extremely good at salary negotiation, and have become a coach and intermediary for people who are trying to up their compensation. Little changes in negotiating can lead to unbelievable outcomes. Here are a few negotiating tactics you can use to get your phenomenal results.

First, think of this as less of a negotiation and more of just an innocent question about a store or restaurant's discount policy. If you're shy about asking, remind yourself that either the cash comes out of your kid's mouth, or their kid's mouth. I don't know about you, but when push comes to shove, it's not coming out of my kid's mouth. My daughter has been one of my greatest motivators, and this way she motivates me to use my maternal instincts to improve her livelihood. Building wealth isn't about me — it's about us — it's about her. If I think of this tug of war negotiation as a way of securing my daughter's future, I more easily get out of my comfort zone and start asking. And when people see your discomfort, sometimes that puts them at ease. You're not trying to get away with something, and you're not being pushy. You're just asking about any discounts or even coupons they might have.

Second, if you are in any way, shape, or form aligned with public service or education, this is a great way to break the ice on getting a reduction on whatever rate is being offered. Military, police, fire department and schools often have standing discounts with restaurants, hotels, and even retailers, and it's usually 10%. (There's that 10% number again).

And even if they don't, about half the time when I ask, the person I'm speaking with usually has some affiliation with public service or education (like their parent or child was in the Armed Forces). If they do, they will usually offer their own 'friends and family' discount. It never hurts to ask.

I always appreciate their generosity because even though the money doesn't actually come out of their pocket, they didn't have to give me a discount. It's a gift, and that gift helps me meet my ability of not letting go of more than 90% of my income. Don't be shy about expressing your gratitude. If it's a big discount, I'll usually ask if I can do anything for them, like let their manager or corporate office know how wonderful they are.

Third, you'll attract more dollars with honey. As I mentioned, I appreciate generosity. Tremendously. I'm very nice when I ask, and I am extremely appreciative when they come through. By the way, I'm also appreciative even when they don't come through because this isn't personal and these aren't their decisions. Let me emphasize that. This isn't personal. Their policies aren't their decision. I know that if they can't do anything for me, then they just can't. If they're a small business, maybe their margins are too tight.

If they're a large business, maybe it's against corporate policy and the person I'm talking with could be reprimanded or fired for providing a discount. So again, I never take it personally. But even when people can't give me an immediate discount, I'll learn how I can get one in the future. This isn't just about getting on a mailing list. I once found out that, at a mall, the customer service counter had 20% off coupons for the restaurant we were at. My sister ran over and grabbed a bunch. It reduced dinner by 20% for 14 people … not too shabby.

Fourth, and only if you're in a real negotiation and not just trying to get a quick 5%-10% off, ask "is that the best you can do." This was an amazing lesson I read years ago in "The Five Lessons I Learned from a Millionaire". And if they give you a lower price or include more in the offer, softly ask the question again. You keep asking the question until they say, "that's the best I can do." For what I've negotiated, usually their best offer comes after I've asked that at least 3 times, but occasionally I go up to 5 times. And no matter where I am at the end of that negotiating tennis match, I'm better off than I was. (Usually a lot better off.)

Fifth, use your smart phone for instant internet savings. I can't tell you how many times as I'm patiently waiting in line I find an electronic coupon for whatever I'm buying. And even if the coupon itself doesn't work (which sometimes happens even if the coupon looks completely legitimate), the sales person usually sees that I'm making an effort and that a discount would really help. I often hear, "yeah, I've got one behind the counter I can give you." Even if it's not for the same amount, it's better than where I was.

And I've got to say this … I absolutely hate paying more for the same product. I've been in line before, buying an identical product to the person ahead of me in line, but because they have a coupon, suddenly I feel shafted paying what moments ago seemed like a reasonable price. And these savings aren't the 50-cents-off-when-you-buy-two kinds of deals. I'm talking 20%-40% off! And if you have a coupon but won't be using it, pay it forward! I LOVE going through the grocery store with a handful of coupons and start putting them on items I don't use. I've even walked by and noticed someone looking at a product I have a coupon for and won't use, and I always offer it. Everyone LOVES it, especially if they weren't sure if they wanted to try the product. I just threw into the universe that their 90% is also worth more.

I like the idea of not only filling up my purse, but helping others to fill up theirs at no cost to me. And if these are grocery coupons that are personally mailed to me, guess what? They track my usage and send me more based on how many I use. Win-win!

Lastly, shop around. At least 10% of my internet time is dedicated to price comparison. Here's an example. I decided that as much as I love real fresh whipped cream, if I kept using a whisk to make a batch of whipped cream, I'd get a hideous Popeye arm. Plus, the organic whipping cream I love doesn't have nearly as many 'whip-ready' additives, and it takes a lot longer to get the consistency I love. So, now I'm in the market for a hand mixer.

I start looking at the ones on the market, and sure enough I find the one I really like. It has several different attachments, yet everything including the cord can be nicely stashed in an attachable compartment. Super sleek with much more functionality than other mixers. But the price is sky high and not really in my budget for the month. So, I start my detective work. Low and behold, a competitor has the exact same one in chrome instead of white, and at nearly half the price. Yes, nearly half. Oh, and it gets better. This competitor happened to be Bed, Bath, and Beyond. What can I expect from this prime retailer? Yup, a 20% off coupon. And although they don't have it locally, the price point pushed me into the free shipping category.

For about 15 minutes of research, I got the model I wanted for nearly 70% off the first place I looked. If you ask around, you will undoubtedly find amazing coupon stories all around you. Don't get me wrong … I'm not a crazy coupon lady (as much as I admire them), but I can absolutely stretch $90 to $100 of value doing this, and I can do it over and over and over again.

RICH TIP$

Hotels: Several chains have discounts for federal and state government employees, seniors, and educators. For Federal and State employees, many think these deep discounts only apply if you're traveling for business, but that's not the case. Unless that is explicitly stated, any person or family member of the person working for the federal or state government can use the discount. Although you may be asked to produce identification, I find that if I am part of their free loyalty or points program, they won't ask. I also tend to stick with Hilton and Marriott Brands due to the ease of canceling and rebooking. Why is this so handy? Because I will absolutely price compare THE SAME HOTEL a few times before my stay. I have saved hundreds of dollars by continuously comparing, booking a new reservation, and canceling the old one. If the price keeps dropping, I'll do it for as long as it does. But with hotels, I try to book 4-5 months in advance, and then keep watching monthly. When the price starts dropping every 1-2 weeks. The price will usually stop dropping and shoot back up 1-2 months before my stay.

Rental Car Companies: Even if you book ahead of time, check the rates a few times before you need the vehicle. I have saved hundreds PER TRANSACTION by re-checking the same company at different times. Generally, their prices drop as the date gets closer, but may start to jump back up 1 - 2 weeks before your reservation. Like with hotels, book your second reservation before you cancel your first reservation.

Restaurants: More and more restaurants are using online coupons with unique code identifiers. They also do a LOT of public service worker discounts. You can usually combine both the discount and a coupon. I tend to save at least 10%. Some restaurants offer as high as 30% off. And watch the Kids Eat Free opportunities. Many of my friends eat out based on 'Kids Eat Free' schedules. Try https://wallethacks.com/kids-eat-free-restaurants/ to see over 100 restaurants where kids eat free … organized by day of the week!

Target: Target cashiers are authorized to discount any item for any damage up to 10% on the spot. (A request of more than 10% will take a manager, but if you believe the damage warrants it, go for it). I have no issue actually selecting a dented box of cereal and asking if they can do anything since the box is damaged. Think of how much your cereal costs. Somewhere between $3.00 and $5.00 a box? That's 30- to 50-cents. What if you're buying something in the $10-$20 range. There's $1-$2 dollars. Every time you save cash on your purchase, you're filling your purse. And Target has an aggressive price-match policy. I was buying a baby shower gift of a pricey carrier the mommy-to-be really wanted. (You know, the kind you use to strap the baby to the front of you.) It was out of my budget, but a quick look at my cell and I could see that a well-known baby product store had the identical item for 40% less. (I would have had to order it, and it wouldn't have arrived in time, but I didn't share that little tidbit.) I took the item and my phone right over to customer service. They confirmed that the competitor had at least one in stock — which is required for a price match — and promptly discounted the item in a match.

Home Depot/Lowe's: These are my two favorite DIY home improvement retailers. Although they are direct competitors, but did you know they are direct PRICE competitors. And not just with each other. Their standard policy is for an identical item, it you find a cheaper price, they won't match it … they'll BEAT IT by 10%. Anything from hammers to refrigerators, I've used this tactic over and over AND OVER again. All I do is pull up another price on my handy dandy cell, and the price is instantly dropped.

Rule 2: Spend with a Sanity Check

Don't tell me where your priorities are. Show me where you spend your money, and I'll tell you what they are.
— James Frick, Lifetime Net Worth $225 Million

N THE AFTERMATH of a financial devastation (like my divorce for example), it's very easy to lose inhibitions and spend, spend, spend. It certainly was for me. The line between wants and needs became increasingly blurry. Even as I was scrounging around the house to find things to sell on eBay so I could pay the utility bill, I had no issue spending $50 at the Disney Store to get my daughter something nice. (And $50 was the magic number, because with my Disney credit card, if I spend at least $50, I got 10% off. The more you spend, the more you save, right?)

Just a year before I started spending with a sanity check, my daughter and I would go to the Disney store and she would look at all of the items in there constantly picking out whatever items she wanted. I was happy to give her anything I could, thinking that as long as there's money in my checking account right now, that I was probably okay. But I failed to consider is that the money that's in my account at this moment it's probably earmarked for bills.

I remember one weekend going into the Disney store with my daughter, and she looked around for at least one hour. If any of you are familiar with the Disney store you know that an hour in the Disney store means you've probably made several laps around the entire store. But what was eye-opening as my daughter could not find anything she didn't already have. And she looked and looked and looked some more desperately trying to find something that she didn't already have.

In that same way I started looking around at stores and realizing that I've pretty much had everything I wanted and really didn't need to continue buying. I began to realize that I had slipped into this labyrinth of retail therapy. I thought that around any corner I would find a deal that would make me feel fantastic and amazing. That deal would let me escape from the misery I was feeling for just the few minutes it took to buy that item. But do I need another blouse? Do I need another black purse? (I hate that my instinctual answer is always yes.) Do I need another pair of shoes?

To be clear, I'm not opposed to splurging on occasion, but it was slowly becoming an unsustainable lifestyle choice. And though I had nearly $50K of credit card and signature load debt (not including car or house), it was all too easy to say "what's 50 bucks more?" I was financially bleeding out, and credit cards make poor bandages. I had to stop the bleeding. Stop the madness. Stop the spending.

There are a few ways to spend on what you need first and what you want second. First, I did some basic math and looked at what my actual income was. Then, I paired that up to my *needed* expenses. Those princess pleasures like a roof over my head, electricity, and running water. For example, food makes the *need* list, but eating out was clearly a want. Then, I looked at what I had left and stopped considering credit cards a solution. Credit cards, or more specifically credit card interest, suddenly was on the *need* list because I had to pay it, but was created by the *want* list. If I fed a credit card, I was feeding it twice - the cost of the item, and the cost of the monthly interest. So, I started building my wealth on a non-credit card foundation. Credit cards can become the quicksand of wealth.

SPEND ON WHAT YOU *NEED* FIRST
AND WHAT YOU *WANT* SECOND

In the first year, I managed to cut my frivolous spending way down. And the strange thing was I didn't really feel like I was missing anything. And my daughter hardly noticed. I mean, every once in a while, she would ask for something that just didn't make the "need" cut, and it's really hard to gently say no. But there are distraction techniques and there are options. And I realized that I could say yes to her now, or a bigger yes to her later, like with vacations, a car, college, and a house. It becomes easier to say no to the toy she's pining for.

To cut down on my spending I visited my library. I'm not just talking about the amazing books and books on CD that are available at the library, but I'm also talking about some of their other services that are completely free. Many libraries have a lot of movies available for free, but they also have them available for download. Another feature that my library offers, and many libraries are going, to is RB Digital. RB Digital is a great way to download popular magazines at absolutely no cost. You do need to invest in some sort of a reading device like a Kindle or an iPad, but the cost benefit is usually pretty good if you really like to download books movies audiobooks and anything else.

But what about that *need* category? I can focus my sanity check skills on that first and foremost. I scrutinize bills like my future depends on it … because it does. Billing is one of those very interesting things that a lot of companies think no one is paying attention to. They tend to inch up your bills by $5 or $10 every few months. Any why do companies like AT&T give you a discount if you register for autopay? Because you're less likely to notice the small rate increases here and there. If you autopay, *pay attention to each and every bill*. Habits take time to build, and if you introduce little changes to managing your finances, over time they become lifestyle changes for your life of abundance.

Remember that change comes in little steps, not in giant leaps. Any monumental or heroic attempt to change overnight will usually fail very quickly, like crash dieting. Don't crash diet your finances. Make the change one step at a time in order to curb your spending appetite for the long-term.

RICH TIP$

Cable: The cable company is a phenomenal example of this. If you have cable service, I would challenge you to consider what you need out of that service and start talking with them about a reduction in service. Also, unless there are certain channels that you absolutely need, consider other alternatives to cable. Amazon Prime Video and Netflix are great examples, but I still love my cable lineup so I have YouTube TV. For $40 per month, I have all the channels I had with cable and unlimited cloud recording. And even when I was with cable, I would call every time the bill increased and negotiate it back down. Spectrum (formerly Time Warner Cable) has this little known means of reducing the bill — go into their store. Their store clerks, who can take payments and exchange equipment, and also authorized to reduce your bill much, much lower than any telephone rep. But with cable, any discount is temporary and will go up in the next year.

Medical: Medical bills are another area there is a lot of room for negotiation. Even if you can't negotiate the total amount, you can usually negotiate a payback option. (But many times, you can negotiate the full amount if you are on a fixed income.) Paying a big bill at once, even if you could afford it, is not always conducive to positive cash flow. I'll talk a little bit about cash flow in a later chapter.

Credit Cards: If you have to use credit cards, and I understand it's sometimes going to happen, examine the terms of your credit agreement. Is your interest rate extraordinarily high? Can you reduce your total interest rate by consolidating all of your bills onto the single credit card or through a single loan option? But more importantly, have a pay-down strategy. Have you considered how you will pay down the credit card over time, and what is it costing you every month that that credit is open?

Reward Credit Cards: When you use credit cards, be sure to use maximize your returns. I know may people who use them for travel benefits, but that would be the best use for me. I prefer to use them for the cash back rewards and hold the cash back until Christmas. This way, I'm never strapped for cash at the holidays. Whatever I earn throughout the year is my Christmas budget. Period.

Rule 3: Make Your Money Multiply

If you don't find a way to
make money while you sleep,
you will work until you die.
— Warren Buffet, Net Worth
$81.1 Billion

M Y DAD USED TO SAY "money is just a tool." And to some extent that's true. Money is a phenomenal tool for getting things like a nice car, a house, a refrigerator full of food, an education (or in some cases a better education), a vacation, an amazing bucket-list experience, and so on. But using money as a barter tool is the anti-wealth. Spending money transforms it into your needs and wants, but doesn't make it multiply. Money as a bartering tool is sometimes essential/sometimes optional, but once bartered away will never return.

To multiply, money needs a purpose. Money needs a job beyond buying and bartering. If your money's job is strictly to become other things, it will never multiply. Never. This was a hard lesson for me to learn, and it took a lot of rethinking and refocusing. Now, I know that if I don't give money a job, it will instantly transform into a thing. Think about it. What happened the last time you got a little extra cash? Promotion? Bonus? Tax refund? Did it buy something? I get that sometimes we need to use money to repair or replace something that has worn out or broken every once in a while. But over time, if every extra nickel and dime becomes a 'thing', these things will accumulate and the money will vanish. Early on, a life of things is counter to a future life of abundance.

IF YOUR MONEY'S JOB IS STRICTLY TO BECOME OTHER THINGS, IT WILL NEVER MULTIPLY. NEVER.

On the other hand, money which is invested will multiply over time. Money which is wisely invested will multiply faster. So what counts as an investment? An investment can take many forms, but over time an investment will yield more than non-invested money. So, let's say you loan a friend 20 bucks, and in a month get back 22, that's an investment. (Now, if you got that every month, that would be pretty phenomenal. If that's possible, go with it!) On my personal quest to making money multiply, I embraced structured investments in all of the following 3 areas: (1) the stock market (primarily though index funds) (2) real estate, and (3) cash holdings. Candidly, the majority of my money has moved into the stock market, with about 35% in real estate and 15% in cash holdings. (I've calculated that 15% is more than adequate to cover my living expenses for at least 18-months. This incorporates my emergency fund strategy covered at the end of this chapter.)

In the past 10 years, we've all heard of great investment highs (like Amazon and Apple) and traumatic market lows (like any housing development investment in 2008). Having lived through the booms and busts in the stock market and real estate markets, it's natural to feel nervous about investing. But for some of our most famous millionaires and billionaires, these two areas of investing are the breeding grounds for what I call massive money multipliers. So how do massive money multipliers work, and how can it work for you?

THESE TWO AREAS OF INVESTING ARE THE BREEDING GROUNDS FOR MASSIVE MONEY MULTIPLIERS

For me, I kept my investments simple and straight forward. I've read a good size stack of books on finances and can tell you candidly I'm no Wall Street genius. I don't pretend to read the financial section like Warren Buffet — analyzing P/E ratios and recognizing breakout chart patterns (although I'm not bad at charting). But I recognized my weaknesses before I started … I embraced a get smart strategy to know just enough to understand the risks and smartly identify massive money multipliers. So here are some hard lessons I learned along the way, and how I found my massive money multipliers.

Don't Trust Blindly: A few years back, I quickly recognized that I knew zilch about investing. Foolishly, I also thought it was beyond my intellect to understand. (Yes, I have a Ph.D., but not in math or finance. I half kiddingly told people for years if I can't figure out a math problem on my 10 fingers, it's not happening.) So instead of doing research on investing, I opted to do research on investing advisors. I literally asked just one friend what he did with his money, and from that overwhelming wave of a single data point, I went with his nationally known chain of investing advisors. Let's call them Edgar Bones. And unbelievably, there was one of their shops right by my house … because they're practically on every corner. I naively handed them the very small amount of money I had to invest (about $5,000), and felt remarkably confident that they would magically make my money multiply. So uneducatedly confident. There were some pretty high fees, but my advisor said, and I quote, "if I can't make you enough money to cover your fees, I shouldn't be in this business." By the way, she left Edgar Bones less than a year later.

Around that time, I was also deciding to make a departure from Edgar Bones. Remember I started with about $5,000. Let's just say that their 'investing' strategy wasn't bad … and wasn't great. But it didn't make up for the not-so-minimal fees they charged my account for every single transaction. So, there I was, a year later, with much less than $5,000. If I kept my money there, I'd eventually have zero. I kept asking myself how this could happen to me. Well, it didn't happen to me. I let it happen. I gave them full permission to do with my money as they desired. When I woke up and took back my money, I lost even more. I "invested" in two separate accounts, and they charged me nearly

$100 per account to close each of them. I was furious, but mostly mad at myself that I had dumped my money here without any real due diligence. By the time it was all said and done, my $5,000 was just under $4,500. (And $500 was a LOT of money to me then. I was selling whatever I could find on eBay to pay utility bills, and this felt like a complete setback.) The moral of the story is if you take control of your finances, you'll learn more and have better control over what happens.

Research: I began doing research on investment firms. I was familiar with several firms, but then I heard about John Bogle and why he founded Vanguard. [In a nutshell, Bogle believed in the power of low-fee index funds, and proved they would out-perform actively mutual funds.] I began a conversation with a Vanguard rep, and was a little surprised there was no hard sale or 'big returns' pitch. It was relatively easy to move money in AND out, and the fees were truly low. To be exact, they are some of the lowest in the industry. I've been with Vanguard ever since. I'm not saying go with Vanguard, but for me, choosing low cost index funds has significantly contributed to my financial success. (I happen to use Vanguard.) Always do your research to ensure you know what you're paying for every step of the way. Invest your time before you invest your money.

INVEST YOUR TIME BEFORE YOU INVEST YOUR MONEY

After I found Vanguard, my research didn't end. In a way, it never ends. I began looking at Vanguard's Fund comparison tool, as well as other sites like Motley Fool (www.motleyfool.com) and MaxFunds (www.maxfunds.com). I also used Morningstar (www.morningstar.com), but Morningstar now charges for in-depth reviews, and I like getting most of my information for free. This helped me to learn more about funds and understand better what each fund had to offer. (Although stocks are also an option, I know my weaknesses and prefer to invest in funds. Individual stocks are inherently riskier. One bad earnings report or corporate scandal can tank the stock price.) Index funds spread that risk among all the companies contained in that fund, and more closely track the broader markets. There is a lot of research behind the philosophy of index funds, and a lot of books.

Diversify: In the latest Peanuts movie, Charlie Brown and Psychiatrist Lucy are in a discussion about what women want. She says, "Do you have a diversified portfolio? What are your real estate holdings?" All diversified means is not putting all the eggs in one basket. Why? Because if that basket drops, the chances are some or all of the eggs will crack and be less valuable. It's the same with investing. If you only invest in one stock or mutual fund and that one tanks, your investment is dependent on that basket, and your value could fall with the it. Diversifying spreads the risk so that even if one basket drops, your other buckets can keep your total investments up. And what about uninvested money? Uninvested cash is absolutely a very stable basket. Although this is a very safe way to keep money, it won't multiply. But you need at least some of your money in the cash basket for ease of access and some stability. This is why emergency funds should be held in cash. In a real emergency, there's normally not time to sell an investment and get the proceeds.

Time is Your Friend: The markets move like the tides — they ebb and flow. There will be the occasional tsunami that wipes away everything on the shore. But over time, highs are higher than the lows. Since the inception of the Standard & Poor's 500 (S&P 500), for example, from 1928 to 2016 the average annual returns run about 10%. That 10% average annual return over 88 years is despite the

Wall Street Crash of 1929 (Black Tuesday) and the housing and stock market crashes of 2007. There is still a net gain. And to counter the deep lows, it means that some years were well above 10% returns. These markets are now experiencing their highest heights. Par for the course, lows are expected. So how do we cope with the lows? I like to think of market lows as mega-sales. If I regularly invest money, I can buy much more during these lows, because the stocks and funds are cheaper per share. I keep buying. Sometimes, as with any sales, I might buy much more than I normally would because I know the market will rise again over time. And because I don't day trade, I'm never in a hurry. As Warren Buffet said, "Time is your friend."

Don't Day Trade: Anyone who day trades will boast on their winnings and underplay their losings. In that respect, day trading is very similar to another past-time I'm not a fan of … gambling. (What can I say? Living in Las Vegas for 2 years, I know the house ALWAYS wins.) For the garden variety investor, day trading is absolutely gambling. Even very sophisticated day traders average less in returns than unmanaged index funds because any profits (whether out of skill or more likely out of luck) are usually eaten away by high short-term capital gains taxes as well as outrageous commissions (around $10 per trade). According to Brad Barber and Terrance Odean, less than 1% of day traders can be considered profitable … and they really have to work hard to get there. According to Motley Fool (www.motleyfool.com), day traders have to earn $72,500 just to break even. That's a lot of trading, sweating, freaking out, and throwing caution and your cash to the wind. Why not just sit back and relax, and let the market hand you at least 10% over time?

Emergency Funds: A few years back, the very wise Mr. E. pulled me aside to have the light and carefree conversation on emergency funds. "Do you have an emergency fund?" he asked. My deer-in-the-headlights look said everything. He then continued. "I slept a lot better at night once I had it. It takes time to build, but you'll sleep better at night once you have one too." So, I started researching emergency funds. Some people say you need a few months, and some people say you need at least a year. You've lived in this economy just as I have. People who lost their jobs during the economic downturn didn't bounce back in 2 or 3 months. I've seen family member after family member be out of a job for more than a year. Some because of the economy. Some for medical reasons. And some because they had the terrifying misfortune of working for a company who preferred firing people a year before retirement-eligibility rather than paying retirement benefits.

For me, 18-months' worth became my goal. And it kinda freaked me out at first, because I initially translated that to at least a year's salary, which it is not. An emergency fund is enough money to cover expenses in an *emergency*. If I lost my job tomorrow, how long could I stay in my house and pay all the utilities? These are the expenses I'm talking about. In that type of emergency, for example, I'm not focused on the expenses ssociated with eating out, going to the movies, or vacations. I am, however, deeply concerned with my mortgage, utilities, transportation, and food. These are living expenses … I need enough to cover that. Most people think of emergencies as a car or appliance breaking down. That's an excellent start, but don't stop there. Keep going until you feel that if something devastating happened, you have enough money to get through the worst of it. At that point, you too will sleep much better.

Rule 4: Guard Your Cash Stash

Money is hard to earn and easy to lose. Guard yours with care.
—Brian Tracy, Net Worth $15 Million

O QUOTE *The Richest Man in Babylon*, "Misfortune loves a shining mark."

There's something so poetic and tragically accurate in that statement. The bigger and shinier the mound of cash, the more disciplined and diligent we must be about guarding it from loss. And that loss often occurs by our own hand.

Looking back, I've fallen for my fair share of scams. Two things facilitate falling for a scam: (1) naivety, and (2) the blind desire to get rich quick. Fortunately, the losses were marginal and completely recoverable. Early on, I fell for the garden variety swindling of buying a tonic to grow longer, strong, thicker hair in 5-7 days. (I, for one, am still dismayed that it didn't work for $4.95/oz.) I've also "invested" in mail order get-rich-quick schemes as well as in-laws needing to borrow money with a guaranteed return. Again, lessons learned very well and not repeated. So, to be clear, guard your cash stash from all of it. Keeping money safe from publishing clearinghouses, politicians, gas pump skimmers, relatives with crazy strategies, Ponzi schemes, pyramids, and the like. And with investing, you must be an extra diligent guard. Here are a few tips for investing that have soundly guarded my cash stash.

Investments must be secure, but not TOO secure.

There is a lot of granularity between keeping cash under the mattress and investing in crazy high risk/reward investments. I have sought investments where the principal is fairly secure, but still risky enough that there is at least some rate of return. Generally, more safety means less return. Still, more risk doesn't guarantee more returns. It could mean more returns, low return, no returns, or negative returns. What are negative returns? That would be you paying for the pleasure of investing … and sometimes paying a lot … and having nothing to show for it. In order of safety, money can be put in a sock, then a CD or treasury note (less than 1% return), then mutual funds and index funds, then stocks, then day-traded, then Ponzi schemes and pyramids. (The last three are usually negative return yields.) The bottom line is keep the principal secure to get a return, but don't keep it in a sock, and don't chase insane returns.

Investments must be accessible, but not too accessible.

I know any given day, if I really needed to cash

out all of my investments, I could access some of it immediately, and the rest of it within 72 hours. So why don't I want it too quickly. Well, let's just say when the market plummets, that is the absolute worst time to cash out. Yet, the reason it's dropping like an anvil on Wyle E. Coyote is that everyone and their mother is cashing out all at once. If you cash out too, you've locked in that loss. But like all market downturns have ever been in history, a downturn is not forever. Time will be your friend. There's the saying 'buy low, sell high' for a reason. When the market crashes, that's the time to buy ... not sell. But, if there's a true emergency or sudden job loss (God forbid!), then cash will be accessible quickly, but not immediately. So, I stick with fund companies that let me move or sell quickly if necessary.

Strive for a better than average-but-realistic returns.

The only way to get better-than-average investments is to learn more about investing. Like you're doing right now with this book. Candidly, this was never my favorite thing, but I got totally spanked because I knew next to nothing about investing. I also foolishly listened to people who, although they are investment professionals, really didn't do very well for themselves with their investments … or mine! I realized I wasn't going to accidentally get lucky with my investments. Finding massive money multipliers and gaining high yields is intentional, not accidental.   So, I had to start on the road to smarter investing. There are several easy to read resources. Kiplinger's is an excellent resource and is often available for free with your local library (which I do by digital download). Vanguard also has webinars with live Q&A chat capability. I took baby steps and took my time, and moved into investments I learned about and felt confident about. I also spoke with advisers at Vanguard and other firms. I also used some great comparison tools online, and used all of the above and then some to form my opinion. I looked at their 1 year, 5 year, and lifetime track records. I spend weeks to months researching an investment before pulling the trigger to ensure I'm going after something with a track record of better than average.

Dollar cost average investments.

Dollar cost averaging is where you invest the same amount of money at a regular frequency no matter what the price of the individuals shares per stock or fund are. If you invest $50, $500, or $5000 per month, you invest that same amount each and every month no matter what the market is doing. Why? For me, there are a few reasons. First, it prevents me from being reactive to market conditions, which is the surest way to buy at the wrong time. I'm not going to bail if the market falls a little, and I'm not going to inadvertently sink all my investment into the highest price of the year. This way, you catch both the highs as they're climbing, and the lows (or share sales) the whole time. You're 'averaging out' the cost per share. Second, I can put my investing on short-term auto-pilot. This prevents me from diverting too much time to chasing share prices and market movements. I need to be an active participant in my wealth-building pastime. If I devote all my time to it, I've just gained myself another job. And finally, it instills discipline in wealth-building. This strategy requires a determination to invest habitually. If investing is not a perpetual commitment, wealth will not come easily … if at all.

Get advice from those who have actually profited from their own investments.

I sought advice from people who were open and honest about their investing. Thankfully, they were generous with sharing their experiences and willing to mentor me. They showed me exactly what they had done and why, and told me how they learned about investing. They don't know everything, and freely admit that, but they know a heck of a lot more than I do.

They aren't managing my investment choices, and that's never what I'm asking for. A mentor isn't there to tell you what to do. A mentor coaches you through your own decisions so you learn how to steer your own investments and your own life.

Rule 5: Make Your House a Cash Cow

Debt is the slavery of the free.
— Publilius Syrus, Ancient
Slave-turned-Wealth
Philosopher

I'M NOT TRYING TO CONVINCE YOU that you should become a B&B or take in boarders (though those are always options). This is a much more direct conversation about home ownership. Owning a home is the payoff that separates the wealthy from the poor, and the owner from the owned. Mortgage lending is one of those unbelievably profitable area of America. Mortgage lenders discovered years ago that compound interest can work in favor of the banks and be virtually invisible to the unsuspecting mom taking the loan. Buried within every standard loan document pile is this crazy sheet that tells you how much you'll pay the lender if you make the "minimum" payment (which is usually principal & interest + taxes + insurance). This is how much it costs you to get the loan. Just for kicks, how much do you think it costs you to take a $100,000 mortgage over 30 years? (Get that figure in your head before moving on.) Now, let's see how close you were. Here are a few costs, (without taxes and insurance) on a conventional 30-year loan:

(1) $100,000 loan @ 4% interest = true cost is $171,870 … and $71,870 is how much is paid *only in interest*. That's roughly 42% of the total loan amount at the end of 30 years. That is what you will, with your hard-earned after-tax money, pay to the bank. And if the interest rate drops from 4% to 3.5%, you will save about $20,000 over the life of the loan, or $50 per month in a payment.

(2) $250,000 loan @ 4% interest = true cost is $429,674 over 30 years. In this example, the interest is $179,674 (same 42% of total loan value at the end of 30 years).

But here's the bigger moral to the story (and you may have already started the math). In each scenario, the amount you'll pay in interest is roughly 72% of the original loan amount. Let me repeat, roughly 72% of the original amount is going to the bank in the form of interest. So, although you're technically borrowing $100,000, the lender is charging you about $72,000 to borrow it. This is the point at which people look puzzled, and are positive my math is off. But that is exactly the point. Compound interest isn't going to be intuitive, even when there is full disclosure in the loan paperwork putting this in black and white. But this is exactly how banks make so much money on mortgages. How do we let this happen? Because as a nation, we're 'ok' with paying crazy amounts of cash if it's translated into a small interest rate and a manageable monthly payment.

In the lender's defense, they are loaning you money for a really, REALLY long period of time. So, they need an incentive. I mean anything can happen in 30 years. (Anything can happen in 3 weeks or 3 months, for that matter.) What is that worth for the bank? What's it worth to keep monthly payments low and let you borrow money for 30 years? With the miracle of compound interest and a gross profit of 72% of the money you asked for, it's worth their while. But is it worth 72% to you? It's not even close to the 4% you think they're taking. But if you don't have the cash for a house, this is how you get the house. But what if you paid off your loan in half the time.

You'd pay half the interest, right? WRONG! At the same 4% interest rate on $250,000, you'd pay $82,860 in interest, or 33% of the face value of the loan. So, it's not half the interest, IT'S LESS! Around now, you might be supposing I'm the crazy anti-mortgage lady, but I am not. Far from it. I've taken many loans knowing full well what I was paying (although in my youth I certainly didn't know and didn't care — just focused on what I could afford in a monthly payment). I'm just giving you a glimpse into why banks are so incentivized to give home loans at the tune of nearly $10 Trillion a year. Because it makes them lots and lots of money. Hmmm…what can I do to make lots and lots of money on my own home?

The great financial philosopher (who did some sciencey stuff every now and again) Albert Einstein said "Compound interest is the eighth wonder of the world. He who understands it, earns it ... he who doesn't pays it." If you take the money you'd save by paying your mortgage payment and invest it, you'd be able to compound the interest yourself. The sooner you pay down a mortgage, the sooner you can start earning your own compound interest on that exact same money. Your house is profitable when there's no compound interest going to the bank.   So how can you do this?

Up the ante as often as possible. Maybe you're getting a raise. Now, I know from cold hard experience that when you don't make much, the first raises go to everything that has been neglected … usually new bras, taking care of a bum tooth, or taking care of a ridiculously bald tire or two. But you WILL make more money over time. Use extra money to pay down the loan. The first house I paid off I did with tax refunds. That house took 12 years to pay down and shortly thereafter became a revenue source as a rental.

Track and Attack. The easiest way to attack debt is to track it and see what additional payments will do. There are lots of free templates for creating a payoff schedule. Seeing how quickly a massive pay-down occurs is very empowering. And if you have extra money, you can see how adding to the paydown plan quickens the pace. You will visualize paying off the house. You will manifest owning it. (Oh, and make sure you specify "Principal Only" on the note section of the check and with the bank. Some have a relatively easy way to make a principal only payments, some make it harder. Ask ahead of time because the default is to credit additional funds to "future" payments and not pay down the principal.)

To PMI or not to PMI? NOT to PMI. PMI, or Private Mortgage Insurance, is a mandatory "insurance" if you put down less than 20% of the equity of the home. Let me repeat that. It's not if you put down less than 20% of the loan value — it's less than 20% of the home value. If you need a loan for $100,000, and the house is worth $300,000, you won't pay PMI. But if you need a loan for $100,000, and the house is worth $100,000, you will need to put down at least $20,000, or 20% to avoid PMI. If not, PMI will charge you a monthly "insurance" of about 1% of the loan amount (on an annual basis). That's about $1,000 that goes to the land of PMI forever after. This money just flies away never to be seen again. You get nothing for it, and you can never get it back. If you have to get a loan with PMI, the split second the value of the house increases and/or the loan amount decreases so you have 20% equity in it, formally request removal of the PMI.

Escrow your own way. If you don't have PMI, and you have never been late on your loan, you are ENTITLED to escrow on your own. In plain English, you can pay your taxes and insurance on your own and not through the mortgage company. But why when it's so easy to roll up the payment? Because they add a fudge factor. They artificially inflate the amount they keep on hand to pay the insurance and tax bill, and in my opinion any money that's mine should be mine to manage. Their inflation is sometimes a few hundred dollars, but could be over $1,000 a year — held hostage just in case they need it.

Ignore previous tip if you're not disciplined at managing money. Seriously, whatever you would have given to escrow you need to keep on hand for those insurance and tax bills. You can't use that money for anything at all, regardless of the emergency. But tax bills usually only come twice a year, so there's lots of time to blow the money. If instead of escrowing it you're spending it, then just keep it wrapped in the mortgage. If you fail to pay a tax bill, the county will impose a lien on your property. If you fail to pay an insurance bill, the insurer will notify the mortgage company of a lapse in insurance, and the mortgage company will automatically sign you up for a much, MUCH more expensive insurance company. If you know yourself, and you won't keep the money safe and in your own escrow, then just let it ride with the bank.

Rule 6: Focus on Your Future Self

The question isn't at what age
I want to retire,
it's at what income.
— George Foreman, Net
Worth $300 Million

W HEN I GO INTO A STORE OR
RESTAURANT, I pay close attention to the
age ranges of the employees. The older
the employee, the more I worry. How much
longer until they can retire? CAN they retire?
Look around. Have you noticed that there are
more "retirement age" people working in fast food
and restaurants, home improvement, retail, and
grocery stores?

I've seen some of the most tragic and outrageous behavior from corporate America in the past decade. People have been fired a year or two before they're retirement eligible. Companies have gone out the bankruptcy escape hatch, dodging their pension responsibilities, yet still paying executives millions of dollars in salaries and severance packages. What will happen to you? What will happen to me? The only sure thing I've come to learn is that if I don't look out for myself, nobody will. Who's looking out for you and your future? How will your future look? What is your lifestyle in retirement? Where's the money coming from?

Years ago, in a famous experiment, participants were given a time-enhanced photo of what their post-retirement selves would look like. They were given these images before selecting how much money to set aside for retirement. When looking at a time-enhanced photo, participants doubled their retirement fund investing. More than that, they put off planning a fun event and even reduced their checking accounts in order to increase their retirement. Envisioning the future can make all the difference. But that vision shouldn't stop with a photo. What is your vision of your future self in retirement? If you haven't thought of it, explore this now and make notes.

What's your budget like in retirement?

Where are you living?

Are you debt-free?

How much do you have invested?

How much does retirement/pension/investments give you to live on?

If you're glaring at the page, realizing you have no idea how to answer these questions, you're not alone. About 80% of Americans have no money going into retirement. But there's good news, great news, and freaking phenomenal news.

Good News

Set your vision, set your path. When you start forming a vision of your future, you will also start laying the blocks of that foundation. Vision started the Taj Mahal. A beautiful concept, a lot of determination, and 20 years later it was a world-wide landmark. Vision is the beginning of transformation. Even from a glimmer of a vision, a step can be taken, and a foundation can be built. And in 20 years, you have your own Taj Mahal.

Great News

Knowledge is power. If you don't know something, ask questions. Ask Dr. Google. Ask people you think are successful. You will begin to gravitate to like-minded people who have their sights set on the future. And when you start asking the questions, you *will* find the answers, then ask more questions, then find more answers. This is how you build your knowledge and create your power. Each question and answer will empower you to set your goals and ignite your wealth building.

Freaking Phenomenal News

You are in control. Imagine me holding your hands, looking you square in the eyes, and telling you in a firm and commanding tone, "YOU ARE IN CONTROL!" Now say it to yourself. You are the master of fate, captain of your ship, and keeper of your coffers. It's never too late to start. I started in my 40's. I got very far, very fast, because I asked lots of questions and I found answers. I didn't start by having the answers.

And I don't mean I didn't have all the answers. I mean I hadn't really thought of any of this and I didn't have any of the answers to any of these questions. I started slowly. I was very intimidated and knew next to nothing about the lingo financial gurus spoke. But I kept asking questions and kept finding answers - sometimes through research, other times from the generosity of amazing mentors. I read articles, looked at websites, and devoured easy-to-read financial books. (Remember, I'm no math wiz. I needed explanations in plain English and preferably extra-large font.) Sure enough, I started to envision the life I wanted after retirement. I started to want to take care of the future me. And I know you want to take care of the future you.

RICH TIP$

College vs. Retirement: Don't sacrifice retirement because you have to put a kid or two through college. The financial guru Mr. E. said it best, "There are a lot of ways to finance college. There's just one way to finance retirement. If you don't take care of your future self by saving for retirement, you may become a burden on your children."

You are the Priority: There will always be competing priorities. Don't put off investing. Let me repeat, DON'T PUT OFF INVESTING. If you have to skip a month here and there, that's one thing. But you need to invest consistently month after month for it to make a difference. And remember, that's the whole way dollar cost averaging works: habitual investing.

Live Below your Means: Live below your means now, and retirement won't feel like a sacrifice. I know too many people with big houses, flashy cars, high-end tech, upscale appliances, and loads of luxuries, but have practically nothing for retirement and are working into their late 60's and 70's. Oh, and their big houses will not be paid off at the point they plan to retire. The rule of thumb is that you can rely on withdrawing 4% of your retirement stash each and every year to live on. In order to do that successfully and in a manner where the money lasts, you have to have a lifestyle that only needs 3% of all your investments. Ask yourself, is that enough? Word to the wise: plan to go into retirement debt free, and make financial choices with that goal in mind. So, let's do a quick math lesson.

What do you need in retirement? Let's assume you don't have a mortgage. You will still have property taxes, insurance, maintenance expenses, some transportation expenses, food, utilities, and probably some princess pleasures. Okay, now let's assume that gets you roughly $40,000 a year.

If your annual expenses in retirement are $40,000, and you withdraw 4% of your investments per year for "life", you would need roughly $1 million to sustain you indefinitely. (This means you need a rate of return of at least 4% after taxes and inflation … you know, so you don't start losing your principal. Principal is your golden goose … it supplies you year after year if you don't disturb it.)

Sounds like a lot, right? That IS the reality. You need a lot to keep you going, or you need to not retire. OR, you might have additional income to supplement retirement investments. For example, if you have a pension, disability, social security, or a part-time job, you won't need as much in retirement savings. Let's say between social security and a pension, you have $25,000 per year. Now you only need to find another $15,000 to cover your annual expenses. To generate $15,000 a year, you only need $375,000 invested and earning at least 4% (plus taxes and inflation).

Rule 7: Prepare to Increase Your Earnings

The more of wisdom we
know, the more we may earn.
—George S. Clason

THERE ARE ALWAYS WAYS to increase your earnings. No matter what you do for a living, you can do it better. If you continuously learn how to do things better, faster, and smarter, you will increase your earnings. Guaranteed.

Opportunities seek out the hard-working, the ambitious, and the prepared. You may find promotion opportunities within your organization. Even without a direct promotion, taking on increased responsibility often leads to increased pay either in salary, bonuses, or both. You might sell more of whatever you sell. You might patent an invention or license a concept. Or you might write a book on the subject. No matter what, if you keep striving to learn and grow, you'll be ready when amazing opportunities come into your life. The Roman philosopher Seneca phrased it this way: "Luck Is what happens when preparation meets opportunity". Too many people hope for the best and prepare for the best. We should all hope for the best while preparing for the worst. I work hard and prepare for both.

Working hard in and of itself is not the way to earn more. On my father's side, my grandmother was a single mother of four kids who cleaned houses for a living. For a divorced Catholic woman in the 1940's, there were few options. My own mother cleaned houses for a living. Each day when my father got off work from his 8-to-5 government job, he would go and help her until about 8 or 9 at night. My mother did this because for an immigrant with limited abilities to read and speak English, limited opportunities followed. And on my mother's side, the family comes from a long line of farmers in a remote village in southern Taiwan. For people with limited education and lots of mouths to feed, there are few options. But in each situation, options and opportunities were born out of work ethic, persistence, and ambition. Work ethic is absolutely key to building success, but hard work alone will not propel you unless that hard work is focused on the right activities and in the right direction. Let me reiterate, hard work alone, although noble, will not dramatically increase earnings.

We've all heard the wise saying "work smarter, not harder" made famous by Allan F. Morgenson in 1930. But I prefer the genius Jim Rohn and his amazing advice, "If you work on your job, you'll make a living. If you work on yourself, you'll make a fortune." To be clear, my advice isn't to stop working hard. Keep working hard. But work on yourself. Work on making your fortune. Promoting yourself and your skillset to advance your position and earnings is essential no matter what you do or how you do it. What would give you a competitive advantage? What would make you better? Faster? Tougher? If you don't know, here are some ways to tap into your mindset to making your fortune.

Build your Vision: What do you want? Can you picture it? Have you planned it? Who do you want to be, where you want to live, what do you want for you and your family? To varying degrees, you have envisioned or dreamed about this, as I have. Everyone has dreams and hopes. But what to do with these visions? A great manifestation tool for this is a vision board. From Olympian Lindsay Vonn to legendary Oprah Winfrey, vision boards are credited with their ticket to success. There's no wrong way to build a vision board. Pick images and sayings that speak to you instinctively. They say a picture is worth a thousand words for a reason, and pictures which speak to you on a deeper level and needs no explanation become the building blocks to the life of your dreams. My first major vision board covered a few deep areas: family, love, finances, and lifestyle. There were powerful images that attracted me and evoked strong emotions. Some were from hand-me-down magazines (as even to this day I rarely buy magazines), others were printed off the internet, and some came from scenes I snapped here and there.

Write it Down to Make it Real: There is something which borders on pure magic in writing goals down. What do you want to do by the end of the year? At the end of 5 years? The sky's the limit … just start writing. You might have heard of the remarkable comedian, actor, and producer Jim Carrey. Had you heard of him in 1985? Probably not. In that year, a young and struggling Jim Carrey was broke and depressed. Instead of giving up, he wrote himself a check for $10 million dollars. He dated it 1995, and annotated it "Acting Services Rendered." Today, Jim Carrey is worth $150 million dollars according to Celebrity Net Worth. Want to try your own check? Rhonda Byrne's, remarkable author of *The Secret*, has generously created a way to give yourself the gift of a check. Try it at https://www.thesecret.tv/gifts-for-you/the-secret-check/.

Writing down our goals and looking at them often helps us focus on them. That leads us to be more likely to achieve these goals. Success can be an awesome motivator as it instills confidence and reinforces our drive, ambition, and desire to reach higher.

Connect with a Mentor: Having a mentor is a huge advantage in whatever your career or passion. You will climb farther faster if you have one. Now, the single biggest question I get from women is "How do I get a mentor?" Back in the day, men got mentors by playing golf, joining lodges, and being in the right proximity to the 'success center of gravity'. Let me just say this — amazing mentors are everywhere. All around you. The universe puts them in your path, and many times we're too shy or feel to awkward to act upon it. I wouldn't have come half as far without my mentors. So here are a few tips for getting a mentor. First, focus on mentors in your career or in the career you're trying to get into. Have you heard them talk? Did you see them (or meet them) at an event? Did you read about them in an article? You can usually find a contact email and/or phone number on the internet. Request a 30-minute mentoring session and say how you know them. (The further you are from having actually met them, the lower the likelihood of a meeting, but it may not eliminate the chance for a meeting.)

Build common ground with a shared interest in a specific area, like your line of work, or a community event or charity. Most people will accept a request for mentorship if the timeframe is short and you tell them up front why you are requesting them. Flattery will only go so far … you need a reason to have reached out to them that makes them an expert in what you want to know more about. Do you have a similar background in your organization? In your community? And when you get an acceptance for a mentoring meeting, have specific questions to ask that will make the meeting valuable.

If you interview them for 30 minutes just to get to know them, this will do you no good. Tell them about yourself, but don't spend the whole time doing it. Tell them why you sought them out instead of others in their field. Why did they resonate with you? Ask them if they were in your shoes, what next steps would you recommend towards achieving your goal. And always be respectful and mind the clock. 30 minutes is not 45 minutes, and it's not 35 minutes. It's 30 minutes. You'll get a better chance at future encounters with your mentor if you are mindful of their time constraints. And if you are offered an opportunity to do something, keep your commitments and don't over-promise.

People who want to work with you will be mindful of your abilities and resources. Be honest with who you are and what you can do, but showcase your passion and desire to improve. And finally, follow-through on your commitments and latch onto opportunities. Otherwise, they may not come again.

Chase Your Dreams without Breaking the Bank:
Once in a blue moon, you hear about how so-and-so mortgaged the house to start their business. This is a very, VERY risky way to increase one's earnings. Slow and steady increases build a better financial foundation than jumping into a get-rich-quick tactic. Borrow money cautiously when financing your dreams. Whether the borrowing is for student loans or business enterprises, what happens if the economy turns south? Can you repay the loans without losing your car or home? One of my favorite sayings is by Sir Winston Churchill, "Gentlemen, we have run out of money … now we have to think!" Are there more creative ways to build your dreams? Today we have Kickstarter and GoFundMe. If you have a product, you can also do pre-sales. Sometimes, you can barter your products or services in exchange for the products or services you need. If you're trying to fund an education, are you eligible for grants or scholarships?

Tiptoe In Before You Dive: If you have an amazing idea for a product, demo it for feedback. You can even take it further by trying to license it with a provisional patent before putting the money and time into patent attorneys or major production runs. If you're thinking of switching careers, see if you can take temporary, part-time, or volunteer position to ensure you like the type of work and want to dive in fully. Years ago, I worked as a temp worker and absolutely loved it. I learned a bit about a lot of different types of work, and a lot about the types of people, teams, and organizations I wanted to surround myself with. I began to see my future differently. I found greater dreams to chase and focus my vision on.

The 5 Laws of Cash

The past cannot change you.
The future is your power.
— Unknown

G IVE A WOMAN GOLD, and she'll shop for a day. Teach her to make gold, and she'll live the life of her dreams. In this life lesson, you pick your path. Hopefully, you've picked so your gold lasts more than a day. Gold, treasure, cash … again, it's just a tool. It can be exchanged for everyday things or extraordinary things. Making money makes you comfortable for a moment. Mastering money makes you comfortable for a lifetime.

Mastery of cash is not a given, even to those gifted with its benefit from birth. Consider the Biltmore in Asheville, North Carolina. The gorgeous 250-room estate is the lifetime testament of George Vanderbilt, born into extraordinary wealth, but with no means of building his own. By the time of his death at age 51, he blew most of his inheritance on the lavish mansion.

Fifteen years after his death, in need of a cash generator, the home opened its doors to the public. They did so as this was an innovative approach to lasting revenue to keep and maintain the estate. George had money, but no mastery. It took his heirs to master money in order to ensure the longevity of the estate. Likewise, Barbara Hutton, grand-daughter to Frank Woolworth and daughter to E.F. Hutton, inherited a fortune of nearly billion dollars by today's standards, and died at age 66 with $3,500 in the bank. Barbara, too, had cash but no mastery.

Like many today, having cash does not mean a mastery of money. When money is simply handed to people (inheritance, windfall, lottery winnings, etc…) they don't have the opportunity to learn the skills involved in mastery of money. Without mastery, people can lose it quickly. Luckily, people who master money can gain it quickly. Years ago, I and a small group of friends were invited to hear the great Jim Rohn speak in person. I didn't know who he was, but when I was offered the chance to hear him speak for free, the cheapskate in me jumped at the opportunity.

In pre-internet days, I had no way of researching who he was, but my friends assured me it would be fantastic. From his first sentence, his mild charisma and quick wit were enthralling. I was captivated by him talking about making and losing millions, and going through this cycle a few times until he managed to snag it for good.

He impressed upon me and the thousand other eager Jedi's that making millions is easy, because it's all relative. He challenged us to try making millions in Botswana. Now that's hard, right?! And despite my financial ups and downs, I knew that if he could do it, so could I.

So how do we lure and keep cash? I learned over time there are five little secrets ... they are the laws of cash. These laws will magnetize your money, attracting it to you and more of its kind.

1. 10% is Mine
2. Make Your Cash Work for You
3. Get Investment Advice from Smart Investors
4. Know What You Know ... and Know What You Don't
5. Guard Against the Allure of Unrealistic Returns

Law 1: 10% is Mine

Gold cometh gladly and in increasing quantity to any man who will put by not less than one-tenth of his earnings to create an estate for his future and that of his family.
—The Richest Man in Babylon, First Law of Gold

CASH WILL PERPETUALLY GROW if 10% is always held close for your future and the future of your family. For every $10 you earn, stash $1. Stash that $1 right away, before you see something shiny.

Can it be that easy? Yes. Wait, let me say that again. YES! Save $1 for every $10. Save $10 for every $100. Save $100 for every $1000. Save 10%, and you'll have the money you need when you need it.

If you're a church going lady of faith, you may have noticed that the recommended tithe is 10% ... which makes sense since tithe literally translates to 'tenth'.

That's because even back in the day when the tithe was 10% of your crops and cattle, churches had to be built and sustained. Growing on 10% is an ancient understanding which has traversed the centuries. Churches, like moguls, know that growth can sprout from the modest but ongoing sum of 10%. You too can build and sustain your estate. You may or may not have religion, but you must be absolutely religious about at least 10% being set aside for your future.

Law 2: Make Your Cash Work for You

Gold laboreth diligently and contentedly for the wise owner who finds for it profitable employment, multiplying even as the flocks of the field.
— The Richest Man in Babylon
Second Law of Gold

IF YOU DON'T GIVE A PENNY A JOB before it shows up, it'll do whatever it wants. All money has a job, whether it's big money or small money, it's doing something for someone. The key is to get it to do it all for you. Cash is a hard laborer.

It's not lazy in the least, but bores quickly. If your cash isn't working hard for you, it will quickly race to a harder task-master. Keep your cash working, growing, and multiplying. Although the job of this dollar may be to pay utility bills, and that dollar is to fill up the gas tank, the jobs of other dollars are for savings and investments. That's when money works the hardest. Cash eagerly multiplies when surrounded by more of the same. Likewise, it flitters free when alone. Build the nest strong, and profitable opportunities will flock to you in droves.

Law 3: Get Investment Advice from Smart Investors

Gold clingeth to the protection of the cautious owner who invests it under the advice of men wise in its handling.
— The Richest Man in Babylon, Third Law of Gold

S O LET ME TAKE A MOMENT on these two ideas: cautious owner and advice of the wise. Cash clings to the protection of the cautious owner. Not the risk adverse owner. Not the 'gonna stick my cash in a sock' owner. Just cautious. Cautious for me means I'm not co-signing on loans unless I can afford to pay the total amount off, because that's what co-signing means. I'm just as responsible as the other person regardless of whether or not they pay. The bank, mortgage company, educational loan peeps, bookies, whomever they are, can absolutely come after me. So, no matter how much I get the puppy dog eyes, 'swear on my aunt Betty' promise to repay, I don't sign if I can't afford the payment solo. It's okay for YOU to say NO, because it's YOUR financial future.

The second part is following the advice of the wise. So, yes, I do have a Ph.D., but I'm the first to say neither a degree nor a certification does a wise woman make. Education (formal or informal) helps you gain knowledge, experience helps you gain wisdom, and a bit of both is a great combination.

Wise is not in the fancy storefronts and wise is not about getting schmoozed by a financial planner. Finding the wise person who is willing to share knowledge and exchange ideas is not easy. But don't settle for less than wise, because there are plenty of people waiting to give you not-so-wise advice. And if you get less than stellar advice, you will get less than stellar returns.

Let's open the debate of fiduciary or not fiduciary. If an investment advisor is registered with the SEC or state securities regulators they are fiduciaries. (fə'd(y)ooSH(ə)rē: involving trust). A fiduciary has a duty to loyalty and care of their clients, and must act in the best interest of their clients or risk being sued. Surprisingly, not all financial advisors are fiduciaries.

Non-fiduciary advisors (like stock brokers, insurance agents, and garden variety financial planners) have a reduced standard, and are not subject to acting in a client's best interest — they may act in their company's best interest and/or their own best interest. Yup, your best interest is dead last if they are not a fiduciary.

But what does that mean? Who can you trust? Look at people who never bring up money (either complaining or bragging). Look at people who retire on time or early and don't work. Read "The Millionaire Next Door" and learn to see who the real millionaires are around you. Don't be wowed by high end cars and flashy spending. Some people have to talk the talk to entice you to their guidance. (These tactics are pretty prevalent in multi-level marketing.)

And don't forget to learn on your own. Like you're doing now. Every book, magazine, blog you read will grow your brain and your gains!

Law 4: Know What You Know ... and Know What You Don't

Gold slippeth away from the man who invests it in businesses or purposes with which he is not familiar or which are not approved by those skilled in its keep.
— The Richest Man in Babylon, Fourth Law of Gold

CASH FLEES FROM ADVENTURES in ignorance and stubbornness. Ignorance is when you throw money away. (Perhaps you're your crazy relative wants to start a business they know nothing about and need your financial backing, if you also know nothing about that business, that's ignorance.) Stubbornness is when you throw good money after bad. (Taking that same relative, after you've invested, he's lost all of your money and wants more … if you give it to him or her, that's stubbornness … aka throwing good money after bad.) We've all had indulgent moments of dropping cash in the pursuit of gold. If we don't know or fully understand what our money is going towards, it's likely to vanish without a trace. Fool me once, shame on you and I should grab my cash and keep it a-movin'. Fool me twice, and that's a tell-tale sign of stubborn.

I often say that stubborn is worse that stupid because at least if I'm stupid, I can learn. Stubborn can't be taught, and stubborn will drive money out the door faster than guests at a party out of food. There are only two types of opportunities to make money: opportunities to gain and opportunities to learn. And if you're going to learn from mistakes, try learning from the mistakes of others first. Those are the cheap lessons. But if you have to learn from your own mistakes, commit those lessons to memory. No matter the depth of your loss, know when to cut the line. Don't let the loss continue to grow — the weight increases and it sucks you down even faster.

Law 5: Guard Against the Allure of Unrealistic Returns

Gold flees the man who
would force it to impossible
earnings ...
— The Richest Man in
Babylon, Fifth Law of Gold

HERE IS A CERTAIN ALLURE to impossible earnings and unrealistic gains. Like a pied piper, people flock in droves when they hear:

'No risk investment' * 'High Returns'
'Pre-IPO' * 'Guaranteed Returns'
'Have to get in on it now'
'Make $10,000 a month, part-time, from home'
'Incredible deal on a low-priced opportunity'
'Hot Tip' * 'Insider Information'

When I was very young, my mom chopped off all my hair because she was just tired of dealing with it. And I really wanted it back. So, my desires led me to fall for a little back-of-the-magazine ad for 'longer, stronger, thicker hair in just 5-7 days'. After sending my cash to the official looking PO Box, I dreamed day after day of long, lush hair down to my waist. Six weeks later, the product arrived. I used it dutifully. As you may suspect, my hair didn't grow and faster or thicker than usual. And, of course, I didn't get a dime of my 'satisfaction guaranteed' money back.

Let's fast forward to the 1980's and 1990's, where the markets were booming and returns upwards of 20% were common … even expected. Those days are sadly gone … unless, of course, you're a credit card or payday loan company. Today, ten-year average returns of 10% are considered very good. Look at track records, and consider risk. If you're being promised immediate short-term returns well above 10%, don't be fooled. First, nobody can promise a return. If they're guaranteed, perhaps that guarantee should be backed with some good old-fashioned collateral. (I personally like gold bars.) Second, remember; "Past performance is not indicative of future performance." Look for aggressive but reasonable returns so you won't lose your shirt.

Secrets to Setting Wealth Building in Motion

The key to realizing a dream is to focus not on success but on significance – and then even the small steps and little victories along your path will take on great meaning.
— Oprah Winfrey, Net Worth $2.8 Billion

I'VE NEVER BEEN THE SMARTEST person in the room, but I'm no slouch when it comes to trying to stay on top of the latest financial advice. I like to think my grasp of finances has vastly improved over the years, so let me just say this up front so you understand what you're in for. For a good portion of this, IT'S HARD! If it was easy, everyone would be a millionaire.

This is not easy to learn. There are a lot of moving parts between market conditions, tax laws, investment strategies, retirement options, cash flow analyses, multi-syllabic words and long division. But the secrets to setting your wealth building into motion is actually easy. Really easy. Ready?

1. Follow the rules.
2. Repeat.

That's it. Follow the seven rules and your wealth will grow and grow. Follow only a few rules, and it grows slower. Veer from the rules, and it won't grow at all. You have the power to choose to be wealthy, and it's a snowball. Building starts slow, and gains momentum over time. Be dedicated and diligent. Set your sights on someone truly important and remarkable — you.

Best Life Ever

*Let today be the day you give
up who you've been
For who you can become.*
*— Hal Elrod, Net Worth $50
Million*

AVE YOU IMAGINED what your best life ever would be? For a moment I want you to imagine how you would feel if you had your best life ever. Breathe in deeply, exhale softly, and embrace the possibility.

I'm here to tell you without a doubt you can have your best life. I am in the midst of a life better than I ever imagined. And I'm not bragging. I'm saying that if you told me a decade ago that this would be my life, I wouldn't have believed it. But today, I'm grateful for the abundance I have. I don't worry about money. I live below my means yet have absolutely everything I *NEED*. (I have most of my wants too!) I sleep well, enjoy my family and friends, travel as much as I want, sip champagne as the mood suits, lavish in great cuisine, and enjoy each and every day to the fullest. I don't drive a fancy car and I'm now dripping in diamonds, but these aren't what I need to feel tremendous gratitude each and every day. I have a financially responsibly life that will sustain me and those I cherish. I know it will only get better, fuller, and ever so much richer in every way possible. I'm living my dream life because one day a few years back, I decided to make deliberate changes. I took baby steps that became the catalyst for the wealth I have now. These same steps now lay before you.

Enjoy every step of your new journey. You're on your way to the life of your dreams. To finding your best life ever.

Recommended Reading

The Bible

7 Strategies for Wealth & Happiness by Jim Rohn

The Five Lessons a Millionaire Taught Me by Richard Paul Evans

The Money Class by Suze Orman

Odds On by Matt Hall

Prince Charming Isn't Coming by Barbara Stanny

The Total Money Makeover by Dave Ramsey

Rich Dad, Poor Dad by Robert T. Kiyosaki

The Secret by Rhonda Byrne

The Richest Man in Babylon by George S. Clason (see next chapter for free download instructions)

The Richest Man in Babylon

If you're now curious about *The Richest Man in Babylon* by George S. Clason, please download it free as my gift to you.

Go to my website, www.RichestMom.com, and under "Richest Mom Downloads" enter this promo code:

RichMom555

Before You Go ...

Did you enjoy this book?

Then PLEASE **share your thoughts in a quick review**.

Your reviews help pay it forward. When we put positivity into the universe, we receive it back. Your opinions matter and I would love to hear from you!

Others need to know what you thought because if it helped you, perhaps it can help them.

Thanks for your support. You're phenomenal!

I wish you the very best in your future. May your dreams become reality. Make it an amazing day ... make it an amazing life!

About the Author

M. A. Haley, Ph.D.

M. A. Haley is an author and founder of RichestMom.com. She has been featured in the national home mortgage magazine "Connect for Success" and been a guest speaker and blogger here and there. She lives in Dayton, Ohio with her amazing daughter and extraordinary soulmate, Mr. E.

Dr. Haley loves educating and inspiring others to overcome challenges and chart a course to lives their dreams.

Need to reach out? Contact me at:

www.RichestMom.com

Manufactured by Amazon.ca
Bolton, ON

21722096R00060